Heartwork
HEALING FROM THE TRAUMA OF LOSING YOUR LOVED ONE

BY MARY BETH WOLL, MA, LMHC, CTP
AND LINDA SMITH, BS

Endorsements

My wonderful wife of 22+ years, Cheri, died a little over seven years ago. She was my best friend and partner in all our life ventures. We raised children together. We bought and sold homes and businesses together. We did missionary work at home and abroad together. We were truly "one flesh". To say I was shattered, in my body, soul and spirit when she passed, would be an understatement. Each anniversary of her death for the next four years was extremely painful and difficult.

When Mary Beth and Linda offered to do some Heartwork with me prior to the fifth anniversary of Cheri's passing, I jumped at the opportunity. "Anything to avoid the turmoil, panic, and sadness of those previous four years", I thought. It was "more than I imagined" or even dared hope for.

The experience itself was intense, yet peaceful. The result was by far the most peaceful anniversary of that very sad day that I have yet experienced. No turmoil. No panic. Mostly just peace, even some joy in Jesus' arms. Try it for yourself and see.

~ Bruce McLeod,
Leader of The Widows Project Ministry to Widowed Men

My first impression was that despite not knowing most of the ladies, there was a comradery and a compassion one for another. I was also encouraged by the peace and joy that was apparent in many of their lives and that gave me hope.

The Lord revealed to me there at the retreat that I didn't have all the facts, so I was able to let go of the regrets regarding my decisions and find peace. There also was a new awareness of how close the Lord was through it all. For me, the retreat was a positive experience and another step in my healing process, so I would highly recommend it.

~ Julie Wallen,
Ministry Widow and Heartwork Retreat **PARTICIPANT**

This weekend's Heartwork Retreat specifically for widows, was incredibly healing, supernaturally quick, and restoratively thorough.
~ Jackie Morey, Heartwork Retreat **PARTICIPANT**

My grief was like a nautical ball that they use sometimes for decorating. My insides were kind of knotted up because I had complicated grief. I was married twice—a wonderful first marriage, not such a great second marriage. There were some very difficult times. Mary Beth helped me to understand it was complicated grief. I didn't know how to get out of it.

And then I heard about the Heartwork Retreat. That weekend the nautical ball got untangled. Now I have peace and joy.

My **LEADER** asked me, "Where was Jesus at the worst part of your trauma?" I realized that Jesus was there to catch me. He was there holding me up by my arm. I now have a whole new relationship with Jesus—a whole new freedom. I'm a new person. I have a purpose in my life. I'm excited about what I'm doing to help other widows. So, thanks again, Mary Beth, for this weekend. It was awesome!

~ Elisa Hawkinson, Heartwork Retreat **PARTICIPANT**

Such an incredible weekend (The Heartwork Retreat). It allows us to be heard and heal...absolutely dynamic for me.

~ Sheila Scarrow-Coverdale, Heartwork Retreat **Participant**

On Good Friday, my husband Shawn was preparing his sermon for Easter Sunday when suddenly he informed us that he was having the symptoms of a heart attack. Despite the best medical efforts, in a few hours, Shawn was in Heaven, and I was a widow.

I shared all the shocking details of my story with my Heartwork **Leader** and **Intercessor**. They helped me get through the trauma of witnessing all the medical procedures at the hospital.

Because my Heartwork **Leader** listened and repeated back the details of my story to me, it brought great healing and helped me stop reliving the events of that awful Good Friday. Also, I was able to remember the last communication and touch between Shawn and me. The very best part about the Heartwork experience, though, was when I was asked, "Where was Jesus in all of this?" It brought tears, joy, and peace to know that in one of the worst times possible, Jesus was right there. Jesus just kept being Who He always is—Emmanuel—God with us.

I am very grateful that I did Heartwork. It was good to really be heard, and it is really good to know that Jesus loves us all the time, no matter what.

Now it is my honor and privilege to help other women with Heartwork. There is nothing like seeing their faces soften because they told their story and someone really listened. There is nothing like seeing tears through a smile when they realize that Jesus was there all the time.

~ Trickett Walters, Ministry Widow and Heartwork **Leader**

**All scriptures quoted are taken from the
New International Version of the Bible
unless otherwise indicated.**

©2025 The Widows Project

All rights reserved. No portion of this book may be reproduced, stored in a retrieval system, or transmitted in any form or by any means—electronic, mechanical, photocopy, recording, scanning or other—except for brief quotations in critical reviews or articles, without the prior written permission of the publisher.

ISBN: 979-8-9926313-0-2

Cover, Interior Layout: Kristi Knowles

Bring your whole self to God

Remember the story

Invite Jesus into the story

New narrative emerges

Give God glory

Dedication

With love and gratitude to Dr. Rita Bennett who introduced me to Inner Healing Prayer at her Emotionally Free Seminar when I needed trauma recovery. Your life's work has greatly impacted my life's work! Though you have preceded me to Heaven, I look forward to sharing with you again, someday.

To Linda James, my dear and loyal friend who, following a life-threatening trauma, lovingly took me through four years of Inner Healing Prayer. Dear Linda, God saved my life, but you helped me to begin living again. You are one of the best counselors I've ever known, and I will be forever grateful to you!

Mary Beth Woll, MA, LMHC, CTP

Acknowledgements

Many thanks to Kristi Knowles, our TWP Administrator and Publisher Extraordinaire.

Sherry Esp, we couldn't have written this book without your sharp eyes.

Gratitude to all the "Heartworkers" - **Leaders**, **Intercessors**, and **Participants** who helped us refine Heartwork by praying with us, attending our Heartwork Retreats, and giving us valuable feedback.

To our amazing Tuesday morning TWP prayer group—Barb Snow, Sherry Esp, Bruce McLeod, Daniel Hazel, and Marilyn Joy Bassham: Thank you for praying us through!

Much love to our Monday night Prayer Shield prayer warriors: Barbara Lee, Don and Sharon Ebelt, Lynn Baker, and Sherry Esp. This special team, along with Caroline Hamilton, have covered us and our families in prayer!

Special thanks to Rick and Cherie Ruchty and the staff of Silver Lake Bible Camp who generously hosted us for a writing retreat in that beautiful setting!

Special thanks to Lisa Madison, MA, LMHC, a valued therapist, colleague, and friend. Your encouragement and professional expertise means a lot!

Contents

Introduction 15

Chapter One 21
   The Evolution of Heartwork 21

Chapter Two 27
   What is Heartwork? 27
      Timeline *28*
      Inner Healing *29*
      Benefits of Heartwork *31*

Chapter Three 33
   What Heartwork is Not 33

Chapter Four 37
   Types of Grief 37
      Typical Grief *37*
      Traumatic Grief *41*

Chapter Five 43
   Post Traumatic Stress Disorder 43
      Trigger *45*
      How Heartwork Heals the Brain *47*
      COVID PTSD *50*

Chapter Six 53
Preparing for Heartwork 53
Qualifications for Leaders and Intercessors..... 54
Creating Connection 55
Repairing Connection 55
Open Posture......................56
Self-Care for the Leader and Intercessor........57
The Story 57

Chapter Seven 59
The Heartwork Procedure 59

Chapter Eight 81
Freedom from Trauma................ 81

Chapter Nine 85
Moving Forward in Grief 85
A Biblical Perspective for Your Grief..........87
Final Encouragement 89

Addendum 91
Heartwork Retreat 91
Heartwork Brief Intervention 101
About the Authors 105
Bibliography 107
Heartwork Journal 109
Bookmarks 115

Introduction

God wants you to be whole—body, soul, and spirit. Nothing impacts our entire being like losing a loved one. As Dr. James Dobson once said, "The mind, the body, and the spirit are very close neighbors. One usually catches the ills of the next" (When God Doesn't Make Sense, p. 15).

The loss of a loved one causes acute pain. Grief is the process by which we move through the agony of letting go of who or what we can no longer keep.

Sometimes, the loss of a loved one also involves trauma by either experiencing or witnessing a life-threatening event. This occurrence can dramatically impede the grief process. If trauma is involved, the impact to the individual is literally off the charts. According to the Holmes and Rahe Stress Scale, losing a spouse is 100 points, the greatest cause of stress a person can experience (Holmes, T.H., & Rahe, R.H., 213–218).

If coupled with the trauma of watching one's life partner die, the accumulated stress is almost incomprehensible. The pain is unspeakable. Sometimes a person just needs to wail and moan and groan. When they reach out to The Widows Project for help, they are often in deep distress. They are too afraid to feel their agony by themselves. They need our help to face it, and the Holy Spirit is right there with us as He prays for us through wordless groans (Romans 8:26).

If left unattended, this pain from trauma can result in complicated grief. Complicated grief occurs when someone experiences debilitating feelings of loss which do not improve over time.

After years of working as a therapist using timelines and Inner Healing Prayer, I (Mary Beth) realized that these methods could help the surviving spouse more quickly resolve the trauma around the passing of their loved one. As a result, I worked with my co-author, Linda Smith, to develop this book, "Heartwork: Healing from the Trauma of Losing Your Loved One". As we have implemented Heartwork principles with grieving spouses, we have seen amazing results in men and women who have been set free from the pain of their trauma. We have observed the distinct difference between those suffering from grief and those whose grief is complicated by trauma. Everyone who has suffered the loss of a loved one experiences grief, but not everyone who experiences grief suffers trauma.

We have found that people who have been traumatized by events surrounding the loss of their loved ones often get stuck in their grief. They have trouble moving forward or even expressing the story surrounding their loved one's passing because often the scenario involves circumstances so horrendous that they are "unspeakable". Even their own brains recoil from these traumatic memories, automatically exiling them to hidden recesses of their subconscious. But recent trauma research confirms that when someone shares the narrative of the traumatic situation with a trusted person in a safe environment, they often experience healing as their brain is then able to integrate memories of the trauma into their conscious mind (Narrative Exposure Therapy, apa.org).

Many books have been written about grief, loss, and trauma. Heartwork is not intended to be a comprehensive work on these subjects. Neither is it to replace professional diagnosis or treatment. We focus on helping the **Participant** heal from the actual traumatic events which sometimes accompany the death of a loved one.

Welcome to Heartwork. We want to work together with God to see you recover from trauma, so you can continue to walk through the Valley of the Shadow of Death until you reach the other side of your grief.

Heartwork

HEALING FROM THE TRAUMA OF LOSING YOUR LOVED ONE

BY MARY BETH WOLL, MA, LMHC, CTP
AND LINDA SMITH, BS

Chapter One
The Evolution of Heartwork

Twenty-six years ago, through an act of pure evil, I was attacked and killed by a stranger who I was attempting to help. Yes, I did die. I was approaching Heaven and heard heavenly music. God showed me many things, then suddenly, He brought me back into my body.

At first, I was just so glad to be alive that all I could do was rejoice in the miracle that God had saved my life. I was so very grateful that He had given me back to my husband and four children.

Within a week, I was back at work, and within one month I was once again singing in the church choir. I wanted to put it all behind me, but it wasn't that easy. I had some choices to make.

First, I chose to forgive the man who attacked me. My husband Bob and I drove to the exact spot where the attack occurred, and we forgave this evil man for every aspect of the traumatic event that we could recall. Because we did this together, I never experienced even one nightmare, for which I am tremendously grateful!

But I did have other symptoms of PTSD. I avoided that area of town. I was hypervigilant, fearful, and anxious. I was constantly looking over my shoulder to be certain that I was safe. I startled easily and was extra sensitive to touch.

My doctor prescribed massage therapy as part of my treatment, but I couldn't tolerate the touch of the massage therapist. The first week she could only massage my hands. By the second week, I allowed her to massage my arms. That's all I could bear. It took me eight weeks to feel safe again in my own body, and eight months to feel safe in the world. I wanted to move forward, but my life had been forever marked by this violent trauma.

My second choice was to deliberately turn to—not away from—God, and to pursue Him for my healing. I never accused God or asked, "Why, God? Why?" I knew He loved me and was my ultimate source of help. But I had to admit to myself that my feelings were a little hurt that God would allow His faithful daughter to endure such horrific suffering.

Then I remembered that just 11 days before the attack, I had written in my prayer journal, "Dear God, I want to know You more. I do not want to be a fair-weather Christian, accepting only blessings from Your Hand! I want to know You in the fellowship of Your sufferings and in the power of Your resurrection". But I did not expect that He would answer that prayer so literally!

I was also comforted to look back in my prayer journal and find that God had led me to Isaiah 54:14-15 which says, "In righteousness you will be established; tyranny will be far from you; you will have nothing to fear. Terror will be far removed; it will not come near you. If anyone attacks you, it will not be My doing; whoever attacks you will surrender to you." Then it happened! The attacker surrendered to the police with a full confession and was sent to prison. Little by little, I began to heal.

One day, Bob was reading a local newspaper when he saw an ad for an upcoming Inner Healing Seminar by Rita Bennett and Christian Renewal Association. The ad said, "You Can Be Emotionally Free!" When Bob showed me the newspaper, I said, "Yes! That's for me! I want to be emotionally free!"

I attended the week-long workshop, learned Rita's Inner Healing Prayer methods, and received a lot of healing. At the end of the week, one of the facilitators, Linda James, approached me and said, "You're not done yet." I said, "Yes! I know!" Linda said, "I want to work with you until you're done." And God bless her, she did!

With the exception of summer vacations, Linda and her assistant, Beth O'Ziel, met with me every other week for four years for Inner Healing Prayer. For a few years, every time we addressed the trauma, I would involuntarily shake inside and out. Eventually, as we processed the trauma with the Lord, I was finally able to put the event in my past. I was able to move forward with my life.

My educational background includes a BA in music and a second BA in sociology. For 20 years, my husband and I served as music pastors together. It was a wonderful and fulfilling time of ministry, but in the back of my mind, I always desired to return to school to earn my master's degree in counseling. Then, this trauma occurred.

All throughout my healing process, I continued to serve the Lord with Bob in music ministry. Finally, five years later, the Lord opened the door for me to begin my graduate studies. Within a year, I was interning at Meier Clinic, a Christian counseling center, where I served as a therapist for about 19 years. During this time, I was able to use the knowledge and skill I had gained from Rita in Inner Healing Prayer to help many clients who had experienced trauma, whether recently or in their childhoods. I was thrilled to see countless people set free.

After six years of working as a therapist, I received training in using a timeline to process trauma. I was amazed to discover that by combining a timeline of the client's life with Inner Healing Prayer, their rate of healing was dramatically accelerated.

Of particular note was a client who was not a Christian but considered herself a "spiritual person". This woman had witnessed her husband's death and immediate resuscitation. He had a long road of physical recovery, but her emotional journey was equally traumatic.

She was able to quickly recover after bimonthly sessions for just three months as we used the timeline alone. Interestingly, her healing was cemented when she spontaneously realized that she had felt the presence of Jesus with her in the midst of the most agonizing circumstances. As we processed her timeline, she suddenly cried out, "Jesus! That was You Who was with me in the ambulance as they transported my husband to the hospital!"

I knew she had completed her trauma therapy when one day she came to counseling complaining of her irritation that her husband did not pick up after himself around the house! That day, she ended her session by thanking me and saying she believed she was done with therapy. The speed with which her trauma was resolved through timeline therapy plus her revelation of Jesus was amazing, compared to other clients who required years of talk therapy. It was truly miraculous!

As I began to develop my own combination of timeline therapy plus Inner Healing Prayer, I knew that God had led me to an incredible process, which quickly brought peace and trauma resolution to many clients.

Years later, I experienced the worst trauma of my life when Bob, my husband of 39 years, died. I was completely shattered. This experience was worse than the attack, because this time, Bob was not there to comfort me in my deepest pain.

I worked hard on my grief recovery, knowing that as a therapist, I needed to understand the healing process so that someday I could help others who had been widowed. I had previously counseled many clients through grief, but I soon realized that until I experienced the loss of my own husband, I had no idea what others had gone through. I even called a previous client who had been widowed at a young age and apologized to her. She was surprised and said, "It's OK! You helped me."

But I found myself not only grieving the loss of my husband but traumatized by having watched the dramatic decline of Bob's precious body, which I had loved for half a lifetime.

It was through the combination of my personal and professional experiences that Heartwork was born. My co-author Linda Smith had been widowed six years prior to Bob's passing. She personally mentored me through my grief. After joining The Widows Project, she and I accompanied countless women across the country and around the world through their grief journey.

Then we developed the Heartwork curriculum and began to hold weekend Heartwork Retreats. At these retreats, trained **LEADERS** and **INTERCESSORS** helped widows and widowers reveal and heal from the traumatic events surrounding the loss of their spouse. The results were nothing short of miraculous.

Soon others were asking for Heartwork sessions in between our planned retreats. Leaders of other ministries were asking us to train their leaders in the Heartwork method so they could help their constituents. It became clear that Heartwork was not only for those experiencing the loss of a spouse, but the loss of any loved one.

It seemed that we could not write this book fast enough as the need was so great!

Chapter Two

What is Heartwork?

Heartwork is an effective method of facilitating the healing of pain from the traumatic events surrounding the passing of a loved one. In our ministry of helping to bind up the brokenhearted, we discovered that some were ruminating and revisiting scenes from their spouses' sudden death. Others were rehearsing the long years of caregiving or the exhausting days in the hospital by their loved one's side. Perseverating on these circumstances was impeding their progress through grief. At the same time, they were receiving "encouragement" from their friends and family that it was time to move on: "Haven't you grieved long enough?" "It's time to build a new life."

We found that they were stuck. They could not receive comfort for grief while they were cowering in a corner, panicked and paralyzed by fear. They could not move forward in their grief because they were tormented by reliving the traumatic events of their loved one's death.

By sharing their story and hearing it retold multiple times in a safe setting, **PARTICIPANTS** experienced a profound sense of being heard and understood. One of our dear widows, Sheri, expressed it this way:

> As we did Heartwork together, I saw Jesus at the foot of the bed where Steve was lying. I knew that Steve was God's gift to me for 52 years. I also realized that I needed to give my life to the Lord and ask Him to help me bear much fruit. I realized that Steve was the one who died, and not me. God has great plans for me. God's promise is that He will never leave me or forsake me. He is continually at my side, every moment, every day!
>
> I will never stop loving Steve, and as Linda says, "That was then; this is now." It is time to move on, run the race, and finish strong!

Heartwork has been a tremendous blessing to many widowed people who are working through traumatic grief. It combines the use of a Timeline with Inner Healing Prayer to bind up the brokenhearted. Heartwork involves bringing God's healing of trauma to the body, soul, and spirit. Through Heartwork, we gently encourage the **PARTICIPANT** to invite Jesus into their terror and trembling. In exchange, He brings them into His safety and security.

TIMELINE

While typical timeline therapy may include the entirety of a person's life from birth onward, Heartwork's Timeline focuses on the specific events surrounding the loss of a loved one, from just before the trauma until the present. Because the **PARTICIPANT** may be traumatized, the **LEADER** assists them by writing down bullet points of the traumatic events as described by the **PARTICIPANT**.

Through the use of the Timeline in the safe and nurturing environment of a Heartwork session, the **PARTICIPANT** is able to access traumatic memories which they have previously exiled to their subconscious brain. In this secure setting, as the **PARTICIPANT** shares their trauma and hears it repeated by the **LEADER**, the brain lets go of its emotional intensity, releasing the **PARTICIPANT** from the fight or flight response, and persuading them that the trauma is now in the past. As a result, the brain is able to receive comfort for negative emotions tied to trauma.

INNER HEALING

As the Body of Christ, we are called to do the works of Jesus, including binding up the brokenhearted.

> The Spirit of the Sovereign Lord is on me, because He has anointed me to…proclaim the year of the Lord's favor and the day of vengeance of our God, to comfort all who mourn, and provide for those who grieve in Zion—to bestow on them a crown of beauty instead of ashes, the oil of gladness instead of mourning, and a garment of praise instead of a spirit of despair (Isaiah 61:1).

Jesus has told us to weep with those who weep. As we come alongside the brokenhearted, we step onto the holy ground of their very heart and soul.

Dr. Rita Bennett, a pioneer in Inner Healing work, defines soul healing or Inner Healing Prayer as follows:

> It is recognizing that through prayer you can let Jesus Christ be Lord of your past—as well as your present. Through practicing the Presence of God and having

an encounter with your healing and resurrected Lord Jesus, you allow Him to do for you what He wanted to do all along. As you are healed, you are then enabled to forgive others and/or yourself, and sometimes God (in what you felt to be His part.)

Dr. Bennett presupposes a triune structure of human beings: body, soul, and spirit. She views the subconscious as overlapping both the soul and spirit.

She defines the soul as intellect, will, emotions, and the subconscious. About the spirit, Bennett says,

> Your reborn spirit is a place of eternal or ageless life, a place of rest and teachableness, one of knowing that you belong to God... the place from which we make initial, vital contact with God, and therefore the place of our deepest fellowship with Him. God's divine nature lives here; you are joined to Him for eternity. (The Emotionally Free course, Basic Training, p. 1-3).

When we are born again, our spirits are united with Christ. As such, our spirits are made whole. It is our bodies and our souls that still need healing as long as we are living on this earth. Heartwork provides healing for the soul by combining the Timeline with Inner Healing Prayer.

We have discovered that as people invite Jesus into the Timeline of events surrounding their loved one's death, they begin to understand that Jesus was present all along. He never abandoned them. They gain a new understanding of God's love and His ways in their lives. Although they may never know all the answers to all the "whys," they can experience the "Who" as Jesus saturates them with a tremendous sense of His presence.

Jesus assures them that He was holding their loved one then, and He will embrace the surviving one now. They can feel His arms around them. They can hear what He has to say. They can perceive the situation differently than they did before. They can know the truth, and the truth will set them free.

When they invite Jesus to reveal His perception of the painful events, they sense His presence and His perspective about the trauma. Then the Holy Spirit shines His light on these dear ones and reassures them, "It's OK. I'm here. I will be with you." This brings them deep healing.

When we bring them into the healing presence of Christ, we are not attempting to rewrite their memories; we are encouraging them to invite the Holy Spirit to reveal where Jesus was during their trauma. Because Jesus is the same yesterday, today, and forever, He can be in the past, the present, and the future all at once.

BENEFITS OF HEARTWORK

As **PARTICIPANTS** experience compassionate listening from the **LEADER** and the **INTERCESSOR**, the following spontaneously occur:

- Healing from trauma
- Increased insight resulting in positive emotions such as forgiveness, peace, and compassion for self and others
- Healed memories associated with joy, not trauma
- Resolved triggers
- Reduced avoidance of people, places, or things related to the trauma
- Integration of memories associated with the trauma
- Distressing feelings released from body memory
- The ability to face significant anniversaries with less distress

As one of our Heartwork **Participants** exclaimed,

> I was astounded at how beautifully the Lord manifested His lavish love and spoke through the **Intercessors** the rhema Scriptures for each person. There was powerful and revelatory intercessory prayer. There were prophetic words shared to bring healing, encouragement, edification, and comfort.
>
> ~ Jackie

CHAPTER THREE

WHAT HEARTWORK IS NOT

Though it is true that our spirits become new creations when we are born again (2 Corinthians 5:17), we may still have some work to do in our souls as a result of injury or loss. The soul (the mind, the will, and the emotions) is where God performs His sanctifying work in us—over time—as He conforms us more and more into the image of Christ.

Heartwork is not professional therapy, but a proven method that allows trained **LEADERS** and **INTERCESSORS** to assist the **PARTICIPANT** to face and heal from their trauma in a supportive and loving environment. Heartwork includes some unique qualities that distinguish it from traditional talk therapy. Heartwork tends to resolve trauma more quickly because of the interaction of the Timeline and Inner Healing Prayer, which brings immediate change to the brain.

Due to the supportive aspects involved in Heartwork such as intercessory prayer, fellowship, and the direct involvement of the Holy Spirit, Heartwork is very effective. However, there are some people for whom Heartwork will not be helpful. If someone has just recently lost a loved one, they are only beginning their grief journey. As such, they are still in shock and will better respond to companionship, love, comfort, and a listening ear. If needed, Heartwork will be more effective at a later time.

While the Heartwork **LEADER** does not specifically inquire about emotions during the construction of the Timeline, the feelings associated with trauma which are stored in the **PARTICIPANT'S** body will surface during their telling of the story. The physical location of the discomfort related to the distressing emotions indicates where the body has been holding the story. By not inquiring about emotions, we are not dismissing or shaming them, but because the emotions spontaneously emerge during Heartwork, in the end, they are integrated into the **PARTICIPANT'S** present reality and thereby resolved.

Because Heartwork is not professional therapy, it is important that Heartwork **LEADERS** and **INTERCESSORS** know when to refer a **PARTICIPANT** for medical, psychological, or spiritual help. While Heartwork may also be used by trained professionals, it is important that Heartwork **LEADERS** and **INTERCESSORS** limit their involvement with **PARTICIPANTS** to the extent of their particular training. Any medical, psychological, or spiritual symptoms presented by a **PARTICIPANT** beyond Heartwork's scope are best attended to by a licensed professional. For example, if someone has a history of complex PTSD (C-PTSD), dissociative symptoms, limited emotional regulation skills, or is actively contemplating suicide, a referral to a licensed mental health professional would be in order, rather than continuing with Heartwork.

Heartwork does not attempt to reframe or guide memories according to the **LEADER'S** or **INTERCESSOR'S** interpretation, nor do **LEADERS** or **INTERCESSORS** induce false memories or add to the **PARTICIPANT'S** narrative. Rather, together with the **PARTICIPANT**, they invite the Holy Spirit to reveal where Jesus was during the crisis. This new information unlocks positive insights and emotions which become attached to the previously traumatic memory. While the **PARTICIPANT** will still have unfinished grief work to do, the perception of this particular traumatic memory will be permanently changed because new neuropathways will be pioneered in their brain.

Chapter Four

Types of Grief

While grief generally takes a predictable course, the impact of grief can vary depending on the circumstances, the relationship to the deceased, the timing of their passing, and the general health of the bereaved person prior to their loved one's death. It can be challenging to know whether you're living with typical grief, complicated grief, traumatic grief, PTSD, or a mixture of these conditions. Here are some examples of the various types of grief:

Typical Grief

Typical grief is a natural response to loss. We process the thoughts and feelings around losing someone or something we can no longer keep. Pastor Derwin L. Gray of Transformation Church in the greater Charlotte, North Carolina area says, "What we don't grieve won't leave" (You Version Bible, Verse of the Day, 9-10-2024). We must be able to grieve so that we can continue to live on without our lost loved one.

Linda's Story

I (Linda) did not experience traumatic or complicated grief when my husband Kirby died. While I was grief stricken, I'd had 2 1/2 years to adjust my thoughts and emotions regarding his leukemia diagnosis. God knows I hate surprises! I felt grateful that Kirby and I had had time to prepare, plan, and process together. We grieved over the fact that our marriage would likely be cut short. We felt sad that we might have grandchildren that Kirby would never meet. We were greatly disappointed that our retirement dreams would never come true.

At the same time, we decided to be proactive with the time that we had left. We enjoyed traveling with family to beautiful places on our bucket list. We treasured extra time with our two young grandsons, Caz and Kayson. With God's help, we courageously faced heartrending conversations. We discussed various scenarios that might happen when Kirby's illness got worse. At what age did he want to retire and begin collecting Social Security? What kind of treatments would he prefer? Should we downsize from a house to a condo at this point?

Even with all this preparation, I was not ready for the devastation I experienced when Kirby died. We thought he would pull through yet another episode of illness, but he did not. I was suddenly left alone to live life without him.

I floundered. I had nobody to cook for, nobody to eat with, nobody to share morning coffee and devotions. Old routines were irrelevant.

Performing the tasks at my job kept me going because Kirby had not been a part of my work world. I could go there and function because it was separate from the grief I felt at home. Work provided me with some relief from grief.

I dreaded mornings because a new day reminded me of my loneliness. The schedule of my job and church helped me to get out of bed six days a week. Saturday mornings were the only time when sleeping in was optional. Though everything within me rebelled against getting vertical, I got up anyway! I made my bed! This was my first step toward a routine of my own.

One month after Kirby died, I was scheduled for open-heart surgery. I was indifferent about the results of the surgery. Going to Heaven would have been just as desirable as continuing to live on earth without Kirby. I didn't have a death wish. I just knew that God would either bring me through or bring me up to Heaven. I trusted Him.

The surgery was successful. After recuperating for a couple of weeks, I went back to work.

My forward progress was not instant, but steady. I got involved in a grief group and a singles' group at church. I started filling my calendar with social engagements once again.

I realized that as a single person I would not be able to retire and continue to live in my house, so I made plans to move. I gradually started downsizing, and after a year, I purchased a condo and sold the family home that we had built.

I started a small group for widows at my church and then learned about The Widows Project. After I retired, I began volunteering in leadership at TWP. Two years later, I became a Co-Director with Mary Beth Woll. We wrote books, started Zoom groups, and brought courage and comfort to other widows and widowers. I had found my new mission.

COMPLICATED GRIEF

Complicated grief, also known as prolonged grief or persistent complex bereavement disorder, is grief that intensely hangs on. Feelings of grief and preoccupation with the deceased are so debilitating that they disrupt the person's daily life for over a year. Sorrow and yearning are to be expected in typical grief. In complicated grief, however, the bereaved person still experiences the same intensity of feelings a year later, as if the death had just happened. They may not be able to accept the reality that their loved one is never coming back.

Many circumstances can lead to complicated grief including sudden, traumatic events surrounding the loss, unmet expectations, a lack of closure, or a dependent or conflicted relationship with the deceased. Some people experience complicated grief, regret, and false guilt when they have been longtime caregivers for their loved one. Also, multiple losses in a short period of time can accumulate and compound grief symptoms.

Some people are predisposed to experiencing complicated grief because of pre-existing vulnerabilities such as mental health issues, a general lack of coping ability, or an anxious attachment style. Someone with a history of abandonment may feel that God failed them, or their loved one abandoned them when they died. This feeling of abandonment can be exacerbated if the loved one suicided. Distorted perceptions of the consequences of the traumatic event may lead someone to blame oneself or others.

We have found Heartwork to be life-changing for widows who might otherwise be stuck in years of prolonged grief. One particular woman, Elisa, was struggling because after being widowed twice, she realized she had never fully grieved the loss of her first husband before marrying again. Her second marriage was not easy. As we worked with Elisa through her Timeline, she realized that she had not fully allowed herself to grieve the loss of her first husband. The events following her second husband's passing were traumatic. Creating a Timeline of her losses allowed her to see that she definitely had experienced complicated and prolonged grief. Here's what Elisa had to say about her Heartwork experience:

> I did not realize the depth to which we would go in the sessions, and I was thrilled to find out where Jesus was as I moved through the grief of losing my first husband. Then the mess with my second marriage and his death and court issues were unpacked. I found where Jesus was through it all. He was with me in ways I had not seen, and I was so blessed by His loving presence. I came home a new woman, ready to find Jesus throughout each day, all day long.

Traumatic Grief

Traumatic grief is what Annie describes here:

My husband Ralph died in a car accident three months ago. I was a passenger in the car. Ever since then, I have not been able to drive. I keep blaming myself because Ralph asked me to drive that day, but I wanted to rest a little bit, so he took the wheel. He didn't see the car coming toward us from the other lane until it was too late. Why did he have to go? I wish it had been me. I haven't been able to sleep for days because I just keep seeing the accident over and over in my mind. I haven't been able to eat. The pounds are just melting off. I know I should eat better, but I don't seem to have the energy to cook for myself. I know I shouldn't beat myself up over this, but I just can't help it. Am I going crazy?

No, Annie, you are not going crazy! Traumatic grief, which is grief plus trauma, can cause complicated grief. Trauma can prolong grief and make a person feel as if their loved one just died yesterday, even though it may have been years ago.

Mary Beth's grief experience was relatively sudden and did include traumatic events. Mary Beth was married to Bob for almost 39 years. Bob was always trim, athletic, and healthy until he began to experience increased fatigue and unintended weight loss. Neither Bob nor Mary Beth recognized these symptoms as ominous. They considered them signs of aging until one day, Bob's skin was noticeably jaundiced. He went to the walk-in clinic that evening and, after a CT scan the next morning, he was diagnosed with cancer. Exactly three months later—to the day—Bob passed away.

Mary Beth's trauma involved watching Bob suffer as she cared for him over the next three months. He endured chemotherapy and many medical treatments until finally, Bob was hospitalized during the last three weeks and two days of his life. He suffered greatly, including a full respiratory code, which he survived, but from which he never fully recovered. During that time, Bob's body changed so drastically and quickly that he appeared to age 30 years in three weeks.

Through Heartwork, Mary Beth was able to process the unspeakable trauma she experienced by watching her precious Bob suffer. When inviting Jesus into the worst part of the trauma, Mary Beth was able to "see" Jesus pick up "the real Bob" out of his lifeless body and carry him to Heaven. After this Heartwork session, Mary Beth was better able to move forward in her grief.

Chapter Five

Post Traumatic Stress Disorder

Some people experience such unspeakable horror in the process of losing their loved one, that it is hard to even face the memories.

One young widow witnessed her husband's assassination when she was just one month pregnant. This unspeakable horror was hard for her to comprehend until she came to us in tears during our Heartwork Retreat. Her **Leader** skillfully worked with her to create her Timeline, because it was almost unbearable for her to do so by herself. The room was filled with God's presence, love, and mercy. God showed them His grace and power as she surrendered all to Him.

On the first day, it was difficult for this young widow to hear the **Leader** repeat the Timeline. But when she invited Jesus into her story, suddenly something switched and she exclaimed, "Jesus was with me, protecting my baby and me! He told me not to be afraid". Then she cried and cried.

By the next day, at the end of the Heartwork Retreat, she said she had finally broken through her denial and realized that her husband's assassination was in the past and not happening right now. Breaking through her denial helped her begin to proceed through the stages of grief.

A little more than a year later, her **LEADER** contacted her to ask how she was doing after the Heartwork Retreat. She replied:

> Since that time, I started to feel and accept that my husband is not here anymore and that all that happened is in the past. I started moving forward with my life. I have a baby who looks like my husband, I went back home, I got a job, and I'm not afraid. I still have some hard days but not like before.

Causes of PTSD include a sudden death, a car accident, a sudden heart attack, a plane crash, a suicide, a violent death, a murder of a loved one, wrongful death, extended caregiving, decline or injury of a loved one, watching the suffering of a loved one, and hearing of a loved one's death.

As a result, they will experience PTSD symptoms such as intrusive, involuntary distressing memories by day, and recurring, troubling dreams by night. They will often ruminate on these intrusive thoughts. People suffering with PTSD tend to avoid people, places, or things that will remind them of the trauma. Sometimes they may even be so traumatized that they forget important pieces of information or events that happened.

The main four symptoms of PTSD include:[1]

- Intrusive thoughts (unwanted memories);
- mood alterations (shame, blame, persistent negativity);
- hypervigilance (exaggerated startle response); and
- avoidance (of all sensory and emotional trauma-related material).

Trauma thoughts hide deep in the subconscious mind, until they are safe to come out. These torturous memories, though hidden, do not go away. Their chains still bind and can be rattled at any moment by sights, sounds, smells, and feelings we call triggers.

TRIGGER
Triggering happens when someone or something[2]

- **T**ouches a previous wound which
- **R**eminds us of a painful experience resulting in
- **I**nward reactivity which unconsciously
- **G**rips us emotionally
- **G**enerating an
- **E**xaggerated
- **R**esponse to our present situation.

---

1   How Trauma Changes the Brain | Boston Clinical Trials 1-27-25, 8:26 PM.

2   Mary Beth Woll, LMHC, 1-22-18.

Touches a previous wound which
Reminds us of a painful experience resulting in
Inward reactivity which unconsciously
Grips us emotionally
Generating an
Exaggerated
Response to our present situation.

How PTSD Changes the Brain

After experiencing a trauma, the thinking brain attempts to protect itself by trying to convince itself that it was not that bad. But, as Dr. Bessel van der Kolk said in his book, *The Body Keeps the Score*, "Traumatized people chronically feel unsafe inside their bodies. The past is alive in the form of gnawing interior discomfort" (van der Kolk, p. 97). He further explains that your body encodes the trauma in visceral sensations imprinted on the nervous system, waiting until the trauma is processed by the conscious mind.

The effects of trauma can be debilitating, but due to the brain's neuroplasticity, it can also recover. Dr. Caroline Leaf, a neuroscientist, describes this process:

> So, neuroplasticity can operate for us as well as against us, because whatever we think about the most grows—this applies to both the positive and negative ends of the spectrum. For example, in post-traumatic syndrome (PTSD), neuroplasticity has worked against the person. He or she has experienced a crushing mental event that fundamentally changed the meaning of their life and altered the brain structurally because of the neuroplasticity of the brain.

As the person relives the event over and over, it wires itself deeper into the mind, becoming a main filter and disrupting normal functions. Flashbacks—reliving the bad memory many times a day—strengthen the circuit, making it worse and more debilitating.

How Heartwork Heals the Brain

In Heartwork the repetition of the Timeline helps accelerate healing from trauma by leveraging the brain's neuroplasticity and cognitive restructuring processes. Again, Dr. Leaf explains:[3]

> The overriding concept is to apply neuroplasticity in the correct direction by rewiring the event with positive thinking of Philippians 4:8: "Finally, brothers, whatever is true, whatever is noble, whatever is right, whatever is pure, whatever is lovely, whatever is admirable—if anything is excellent or praiseworthy—think about such things." Thus, the person consciously chooses, preferably under the leading of the Holy Spirit, to bring the memory into consciousness where it becomes plastic enough to actually be changed.
>
> This means the physical substrate of the memory becomes weakened, vulnerable, malleable, and enabled to be manipulated. The person then chooses to replace the crushing mental event with the implanted Word of God which saves the soul (James 1:21). The person, as though an outsider looking in through a window, will observe the toxic, traumatic memory as a weakening and dying

---

3   Switch on Your Brain, p. 63-64.

experience but, at the same time, observe the new healthy experience that is growing.

Neurons that don't get enough signal (the rehearsing of the negative event) will start firing apart, wiring apart, pulling out, and destroying the emotion attached to the trauma. In addition, certain chemicals like oxytocin (bonds and remolds chemicals), dopamine (increases focus and attention), and serotonin (increases feelings of peace and happiness) all start flowing around the traumatic thoughts, weakening them even more. This all helps to disconnect and desynchronize the neurons; if they stop firing together, they will no longer wire together. This leads to wiping out or popping those connections and rebuilding new ones.

Recent research on trauma recovery indicates that PTSD is most successfully resolved when the client is in a relaxed physical state as they share their narrative. Heartwork differs from progressive physical relaxation techniques and guided imagery in typical PTSD/ timeline therapy. The relaxed atmosphere of Heartwork is a result of the prayer by the leadership before the session, the love of God expressed through the **LEADER** and **INTERCESSOR**, the use of the Armor of God Prayer, the Inner Healing Prayer, and the presence of the Holy Spirit as He interacts with the **LEADER**, **INTERCESSOR**, and **PARTICIPANT**.

The **LEADER** assists the **PARTICIPANT** in creating the Timeline of the traumatic events surrounding the death of their loved one. This activates the hippocampus, the memory center of the brain, to better structure the fragmented memories which have been frozen in the subconscious mind. Further repetitions of the Timeline bring the memories into the consciousness of the **PARTICIPANT** where they are accessible for change. This repetition in a safe and structured environment calms the amygdala, the alarm system of the brain, thus diminishing the fear response. As the brain learns that the trauma is no longer threatening the **PARTICIPANT**, it is neurologically rewired from trauma dominance to resilience and comfort.

By combining the repetition of the Timeline with Inner Healing Prayer, Heartwork aids in restructuring the way the brain processes the trauma, paving the way for long-term healing. Jesus, Himself, powerfully reframes and, in effect, heals the memory by revealing His presence. The **INTERCESSOR'S** closing prayer then seals the healing by further interaction with the Holy Spirit.

Teresa's testimony is a perfect example of how Heartwork brings healing to PTSD:

Teresa was at work when she got the call that there had been an accident at home. Though she did not know details, she knew in her gut that her husband Gary had died. When she was finally able to leave work, she arrived home to find her husband pinned by his truck and their son desperately trying to free him. Emergency personnel arrived, but all their efforts were to no avail.

Knowing that Gary was gone and there was nothing she could do for him, Teresa was more concerned about protecting her son from the trauma than caring for her own emotional state. It wasn't until later that she was able to grieve privately.

Through Heartwork, Teresa was able to tell the horrific details of the story in a safe and loving environment. The nightmares decreased, and after applying herself to not only Heartwork, but a support group and other personal efforts, Teresa's trauma symptoms decreased dramatically. In her case, she will need more Heartwork sessions to completely resolve the trauma, but she has been able to move forward significantly.

COVID PTSD

Many people have experienced PTSD related to losing loved ones through the COVID pandemic. Karen was suddenly separated from Phil, her husband of forty-nine years, when they called 911. The first responders took him away by ambulance. After that, the hospital did not allow her to visit Phil, so she only spoke to him briefly by FaceTime. He was a doctor, and she was a nurse. Even so, because he had COVID, he was treated with the hospital's standard COVID protocol and was not allowed to continue a prescribed COVID medication. For several days, the hospital also failed to give another necessary medication. Karen was not allowed to be at Phil's side or provide any input toward his medical care. She believed that this hastened his death which otherwise might have been prevented with proper medical treatment.

Heartwork provided her with the opportunity to express her feelings of anger towards and betrayal by the medical system. She also processed the trauma she experienced by being separated from Phil between the time she called 911 until the point when he could no longer respond to her. After experiencing Heartwork, Karen finally came to a sense of peace. Because her husband was a believer in Christ, Karen knew that God Himself—not the hospital—had numbered his days.

The COVID pandemic multiplied cases of PTSD as:
- People were not able to care for, visit, or say "Goodbye" to their loved one, leaving many to die alone.
- Hospitals' one-size-fits-all protocol assumed the patient

would die.

- Some may have experienced a wrongful death due to the COVID protocol.
- COVID vaccines may have resulted in injury or death.
- No funerals were allowed.
- Uncertainty about or obfuscation of facts around COVID deaths may have exacerbated PTSD symptoms.
- Imposed isolation during the loved one's illness and after their death prevented healing from PTSD.

Heartwork has allowed many **PARTICIPANTS** the safety and security to bring their formerly unspeakable stories into the light of Jesus' healing presence. This has released them from trauma and helped them to move forward in their grief process.

Chapter Six

Preparing for Heartwork

To our potential **Leaders** and **Intercessors**, we would like to say, "Thank you!" Thank you so much for answering God's call to help set the captives free. This takes great love, tenderness, and compassion. It also takes tremendous courage to walk with a person into the darkest places of their hearts and minds.

Isaiah 61:1b says that Jesus came to proclaim freedom for the captives and release from darkness for the prisoners. You are among the spiritual special forces, called by God to accept the bold mission of rescuing a soul held hostage by the fear and terror of trauma, but as in any strategic operation, you do not enter this mission alone. Jesus deploys us two by two, and the Holy Spirit is the Commander in Chief.

Trauma hostages are captive and unable to free themselves. As a strategic negotiator, the **Leader's** voice is the only one the **Participant** hears. While the **Intercessor** prays silently, binding the enemy, the spiritual special forces can then set the captives free.

To our potential **PARTICIPANTS**, we would like to say, "You're gonna make it!" You have come to a safe and welcoming community of believers in Jesus Christ who love Him and love you. Hebrews 4:15 tells us that Jesus is "touched with the feeling of our infirmities." This includes the jumble of feelings that we experience after a trauma. Jesus is here to meet you in the midst of that tangled mess of fear and distressing memories. There is healing from trauma. With Jesus it is possible. You don't have to live with this phantom of fear any longer. Jesus can set you free, and Heartwork is here to help facilitate your healing.

QUALIFICATIONS FOR LEADERS AND INTERCESSORS

- A Mature Christian - Because the **LEADER** and **INTERCESSOR** will assist **PARTICIPANTS** through the trauma of a major life challenge, it is important that they have a well-developed, biblically-grounded relationship with God.

- Strong and Steady - Because the **LEADER** and **INTERCESSOR** will be trustworthy allies to those in crisis, they will need to be encouraging and stable, not experiencing serious emotional or psychological problems.

- A "People Person" - Because Heartwork is all about helping others, the **LEADER** and **INTERCESSOR** will need to exhibit an authentic love for people.

- A Team Player - Because Heartwork involves a ministry team, while having strong leadership traits, the **LEADER** and **INTERCESSOR** must also demonstrate a cooperative, respectful attitude when relating to others.

- Trustworthy - Because the **LEADER** and **INTERCESSOR** will be entrusted with deeply personal information, they must be able to protect the confidentiality of the **PARTICIPANT**. The only exception to this rule is when a **LEADER** or **INTERCESSOR** has reason to believe that a **PARTICIPANT** is an immediate danger to oneself or others. In such a situation, the **LEADER** is to call 911, then report this to the staff if in a Heartwork Retreat setting.

CREATING CONNECTION

In my many years as a clinical therapist, I, Mary Beth, experienced the power of the therapeutic connection. Even though the first session included intake paperwork, insurance, and other necessary tasks, my most important task was to provide a welcoming, loving, and supportive atmosphere in which the client could feel safe. The level of our connection determined whether there would ever be a second session. As therapy progressed, it was critical to maintain this therapeutic alliance in order for the client to feel safe enough to open up and share personal thoughts and emotions with me.

In therapy, the outcome depends largely on the therapeutic bond, regardless of the treatment modality. In Heartwork, the bond that the **LEADER** and **INTERCESSOR** cultivate with the **PARTICIPANT** will also facilitate their connection with Jesus. When they connect, Jesus will bring permanent healing to the **PARTICIPANT**.

REPAIRING CONNECTION

Because of its significance, building and maintaining a close connection with the **PARTICIPANT** can pose challenges if the **LEADER** experiences resistance or if trust is ruptured. It is important to stop and address these issues right away so that the bonding can be repaired and Heartwork can continue.

Some **PARTICIPANTS** may demonstrate resistance if the pace of the reading the Timeline feels too fast for them. Rushing the reading of the Timeline can result in emotional flooding. In such a situation, it is important to stop and ask the **Participant,** "How was the pace of my reading for you?" The **Leader** can then adjust accordingly.

Some **Participants** may attempt to mask their anxiety by talking during the reading of the Timeline. While it is important for the **Participant** to be able to correct any errors in the Timeline, the **Leader** must resist the temptation to enter into a discussion because doing so will interfere with the integration of the memories.

Also, the **Leader, Intercessor,** and **Participant** will benefit most by agreeing ahead of time not to continue the Heartwork discussion into the break. They will all benefit from lighter conversations during the break in order to be refreshed for the next session.

Open Posture

During Heartwork, it is important for the **Leader** to bear in mind that the right hemisphere of the **Participant's** brain will be involved in recalling the emotional intensity of the memory, while their left hemisphere will help them identify the sequence of events. For this reason, the **Leader** encourages the **Participant** not to cross arms, hands, or legs in a self-protective posture, but to keep the midline of the body open. The open body posture encourages right brain/left brain interaction, called bilateral brain communication. This is necessary to:

- Allow the **Participant** to relax and be more aware of their body.
- Decrease defensive resistance as memories emerge.

- Keep the **Participant** grounded in their body rather than dissociating into their emotions.

- Integrate past experiences into the present.

Self-Care for the Leader and Intercessor

Heartwork **Leaders** and **Intercessors** can be vulnerable to vicarious trauma if they allow themselves to internalize the **Participant's** pain. Heartwork **Leaders** and **Intercessors** can protect themselves by:

- praying together for each other and the **Participant** before the **Participant** arrives,

- taking brief breaks between each telling of the Timeline,

- asking themselves after the session, "How do I feel right now?" "Is there any tension in my body?" "Did the **Participant's** story trigger anything in me?",

- debriefing and praying with each other after the **Participant** leaves, and

- limiting the total number of Heartwork sessions per day.

The Story

The story of the **Participant's** trauma is extremely personal. Even though it may be traumatic, it is still precious because they experienced it at the very core of their being. When creating a Timeline together with a **Participant**, it is important for the **Leader** to consider the **Participant's** heart as holy ground. This requires deep trust in the Lord, the **Leader**, and the **Intercessor**. As Psalm 62:8a says, "Trust in Him at all times, you people; pour out your hearts to Him."

In order to share the Timeline with the **Leader**, it is critical for the **Participant** to feel safe, supported, seen, and heard. It is within this atmosphere of patient and loving acceptance that we assist the **Participants** in creating the Timeline. On rare occasions, a **Participant** may come with the Timeline already prepared. It is recommended, however, that the **Participant** wait to share the details of the trauma within the loving support of the Heartwork **Leader** and **Intercessor**.

Chapter Seven

The Heartwork Procedure

The following pages are a step-by-step guide to doing Heartwork. It is ideal, if possible, that **Participants** familiarize themselves with *Heartwork: Healing from the Trauma of Losing Your Loved One* before coming to a Heartwork session. If time or circumstances do not permit this, it is still recommended that **Participants** bring their own copies of the Heartwork book to their sessions. The **Leader** will then record the events of the **Participant's** Timeline in their books for them to have a permanent record of their Timeline and their Heartwork session.

Should **Participants** require more than one session to resolve the trauma (which is not unusual), or if the Heartwork session is within a retreat setting (in which there are typically three sessions), **Participants** can bring their Heartwork books to the next session for the **Leader's** use in reading the Timeline.

Following the Heartwork session, it will be helpful for **Participants** to record their thoughts and feelings in the Heartwork Journal pages provided at the end of this book. Prayerfully journaling soon after the session will increase the **Participant's** insight, accelerating their healing from trauma, and allowing them to move forward in their grief process.

OUTLINE

Orientation to Heartwork

Opening the Session
- Prayer
- Armor of God Prayer

Building the Timeline

Transition #1
- Check-in and Physical Response #1

The Second Telling of the Timeline
- Preparation
- Telling Back the Timeline

Transition #2
- Check-in and Physical Response #2

The Third Telling of the Timeline
- Preparation
- Telling Back the Timeline

Transition #3
- Check-in and Physical Response #3

Inner Healing
- Inner Healing Prayer
- Going Deeper

Transition #4
- Check-in and Physical Response #4
- Progressive Physical Responses

Intercessory Prayer

Sealing Prayer

PARTICIPANT'S NAME:_____

PHONE:_____

LEADER'S NAME: _____

INTERCESSOR'S NAME: _____

DATE: _____

OPENING THE SESSION

PRAYER
The **LEADER** invites the Holy Spirit to be present in the session as they pray for the **PARTICIPANT**. Include the "Armor of God Prayer" below, as referenced in Ephesians 6:10-17.

Armor of God Prayer

From Ephesians 6: 10-17

I take up the Belt of Truth.
Thank You that Your Word is Truth.
You are the Way, the Truth, and the Life.

I put on the Breastplate of Righteousness.
I thank You that I am the Righteousness
of God in Christ Jesus.

I put on the Shoes of the Preparation
of the Gospel of Peace.
I choose to go where You want me to go.

I take up the Shield of Faith
with which I quench all the fiery darts
of the wicked one.

I put on the Helmet of Salvation.
Thank you, Lord, that You have given me
the very Mind of Christ.

I take up the Sword of the Spirit,
which is the Word of God, sharper than any two-edged sword,
dividing the soul and spirit.

In Jesus' Mighty Name,

Amen

Orientation to Heartwork

Heartwork is a tool to help the **Participant** resolve traumatic events experienced during the passing of their loved one. It differs from talk therapy in that Heartwork focuses on creating and repeating a Timeline of events which occurred immediately before, during, and after the crisis, and up to the present. The purpose of Heartwork is not to process the **Participant's** emotions and thoughts—valuable as they are—but to integrate the events of the trauma into their present reality. Heartwork convinces the **Participant's** brain that the trauma is in the past and not happening right now.

Each Heartwork Team involves three people: the **Participant**, the **Leader**, and the **Intercessor**. Together, the **Participant** and **Leader** create a Timeline of the crisis while the **Intercessor** prays for the Team.

While the **Leader** creates the Timeline, it is important to leave space between the lines of the recorded memories. As the **Participant** begins to integrate the trauma into their consciousness, they will remember more details. It is not our purpose to create a comprehensive Timeline, but to allow for peripheral memories that begin to integrate.

Because the **Participant's** brain will be working hard to connect left-brain events with right-brain emotions, it is critical that the **Intercessor** prays silently, and the **Leader's** voice is the *only one* the **Participant** hears.

As the **Intercessor** prays silently during the session, they write down any impressions they receive from the Holy Spirit. The **Intercessor** will have an opportunity to share these impressions in prayer with the **Participant** at the end of the session. The **Leader** will record the **Intercessor's** final prayer on the **Participant's** phone.

BUILDING THE TIMELINE

BEFORE THE CRISIS

The **LEADER** will say, "Please tell us what was happening immediately before the crisis (i.e., working, going to school, family life, etc.)."

_____

_____

_____

_____

THE FIRST SIGN OF CRISIS

"What and when was the first sign of crisis?"

_____

_____

_____

_____

TIMELINE

WHEN?   WHAT HAPPENED?

When?   What happened?

When?   What happened?

When? What happened?

AFTER THE CRISIS

"What main events happened between then and now?"

WHEN?   **WHAT HAPPENED?**

_____

_____

_____

_____

_____

_____

_____

_____

_____

_____

_____

_____

_____

_____

_____

_____

THIS CONCLUDES THE FIRST TELLING OF THE TIMELINE.

TRANSITION #1

The **LEADER** asks: "How was that for you to share your story with me?"

_____

_____

_____

_____

CHECK-IN #1

The **LEADER** asks the **PARTICIPANT**:

"What was the worst part of the crisis?"

_____

_____

_____

_____

"Now, close your eyes and think about your body from head to toe. When you recall the worst part of the crisis, where do you feel it in your body?"

PHYSICAL RESPONSE #1 _____

(**LEADER**: *Do **not** ask the **PARTICIPANT** about their emotions because that would distract them from processing their Timeline. We care about their emotions, but the purpose of Heartwork is to integrate the past with the present in such a way that the **PARTICIPANT'S** brain understands that the crisis is not happening now.*)

The Second Telling of the Timeline

Preparation

The **Leader** instructs the **Participant** to relax for a moment. The **Leader** prepares the **Participant** by doing the following:

1. Ask the **Participant** to uncross their legs, arms, and hands. Explain that Heartwork involves using both the left and right brain. The left brain focuses on the Timeline, while the right brain focuses on emotions. Heartwork facilitates communication between the various parts of the brain in order to integrate the trauma, convincing the unconscious brain that the **Participant** is not in danger right now.

   Uncrossing legs, etc., allows communication to flow more freely between the left and right hemispheres of the brain.

2. The **Leader** explains, "Next, I'm going to read your Timeline back to you. Feel free to close your eyes or keep them open. As you hear your story, you will see a video of your Timeline in your mind."

3. The **Leader** requests, "Tell me when you are ready to begin."

Telling Back the Timeline

When the **Participant** is ready, the **Leader** reads the Timeline to them while remaining mindful of pacing their reading for the **Participant's** comfort. The **Leader** will gauge their speed according to the **Participant's** non-verbal responses, i.e., nods, "uh huh," etc.

This concludes the Second Telling of the Timeline.

TRANSITION #2

The **LEADER** asks: "How was that for you to hear me reading your story to you? And how was the pace of my reading?"

_____

_____

_____

_____

CHECK-IN #2

The **LEADER** asks the **PARTICIPANT**: "Close your eyes and think about your body from head to toe. When you think about the worst part of the crisis, where do you feel it in your body now?"

PHYSICAL RESPONSE #2 _____

(**LEADER**: *If Physical Response #2 is in the same body part as in Physical Response #1, compare the degree of intensity between the two responses on a scale from 1-10.)*

The Third Telling of the Timeline

Preparation

The **Leader** instructs the **Participant** to relax for a moment. The **Leader** prepares the **Participant** by doing the following:

1. Remind the **Participant** to uncross their arms, legs, and hands.

2. Tell the **Participant**, "Let me know when you are ready to begin."

Telling Back the Timeline

When the **Participant** is ready, the **Leader** reads the Timeline back to them, remaining mindful of their pace according to the **Participant's** non-verbal responses.

Transition #3

The **Leader** asks: "How was that for you to hear me reading your story to you? And how was the pace of my reading?"

_____

_____

_____

_____

CHECK-IN #3

The **LEADER** asks the **PARTICIPANT**: "Close your eyes and think about your body from head to toe. When you think about the worst part of the crisis, where do you feel it in your body now?"

PHYSICAL RESPONSE #3 _____

THIS CONCLUDES THE THIRD TELLING OF THE TIMELINE.

Inner Healing

Before praying, ask the **PARTICIPANT** to silently read the following Inner Healing Prayer.

The **LEADER** says, "If you agree with this prayer, we will now invite Jesus into your Timeline as you read this Inner Healing Prayer[4] aloud."

Inner Healing Prayer

Dear Father God,

I yield my will to You. I give You permission to go to any level within me to heal, cleanse, and restore according to Your truth.

To the best of my ability, I invite You to be my Lord, unconditionally. Please be Lord of my subconscious, as well as my conscious mind.

I renounce every false teaching and attitude and ask You to cleanse and protect me with Jesus' blood.

I cast down every wrong imagination and everything that exalts itself against the knowledge of God, and I take every thought captive to the obedience of the Lord Jesus Christ. (2 Corinthians 10:5).

Thank You, Lord God.

In Jesus' Name, AMEN.

---

4   Yielding Your Will to God and Cleansing Imagination Prayer, Rita Bennett, Emotionally Free Course, Basic Prayer Book, p. 20.

Going Deeper

The **Leader** states, "Because Jesus is the same yesterday, today, and forever, we know that He was with you during the crisis. Through the Inner Healing Prayer, you have invited Him into our session. Let's ask the Holy Spirit to show you where Jesus was during the crisis. Let's wait patiently to hear what the Holy Spirit wants to show you."

After a period of waiting, the **Leader** asks: "Where was Jesus during the crisis?"

_____

_____

_____

_____

"What was Jesus doing?"

_____

_____

_____

_____

"What did Jesus say?"

_____

_____

_____

_____

TRANSITION #4

The **LEADER** asks: "How was that for you to see Jesus in your experience?"

_____

_____

_____

_____

CHECK-IN #4

The **LEADER** asks the **PARTICIPANT**: "Close your eyes and think about your body from head to toe. When you think about the worst part of the crisis, where do you feel it in your body now?"

PHYSICAL RESPONSE #4 _____

The **LEADER** records all four physical responses below:

1. _____
2. _____
3. _____
4. _____

INTERCESSORY PRAYER

The **LEADER** explains, "We will now invite the **INTERCESSOR** to pray for the **PARTICIPANT**."

During this prayer, the **INTERCESSOR** prays according to what the Holy Spirit has been communicating to them throughout the Heartwork session.

- The **LEADER** records the **INTERCESSOR'S** prayer on the **PARTICIPANT'S** phone for them to keep.
- If the **PARTICIPANT** did not bring their phone, the **LEADER** will record the **INTERCESSOR'S** prayer and send it to the **PARTICIPANT**.

SEALING PRAYER

The **LEADER** closes the Heartwork session with this Sealing Prayer[5]:

> "That which has been done in Jesus' Name and to His glory cannot be undone. I decree this and seal this prayer in the Name of the Father, Son, and Holy Spirit."

---

5   Sealing Prayer, Dr. Rita Bennett, Emotionally Free Course, Basic Prayer Book, p. 55.

Chapter Eight

Freedom from Trauma

When **Participants** sit with a loving Heartwork **Leader** and **Intercessor**, they are encouraged to welcome Jesus into the session. As a result, they feel safe enough to begin to unpack their narrative. Often people will say about their unspeakable story, "I've never told anybody this before, but..."

We have walked many widows and widowers through the Heartwork process. Almost without exception, people come to us weighed down, afraid, sad, and grieving. And they leave feeling like a huge weight has been lifted off their shoulders. Their faces are bright and light, and they say things like "I feel like a new person!"

Many women and men report that Heartwork is life changing. Some, like Sheila, felt that her life was over when her spouse died. She had nothing to live for without her spouse. Sheila had been a long-time caregiver for her husband Johnny who had HHT, a rare blood disorder. This sent him to the hospital countless times, so Sheila and Johnny did face some preparatory grieving. However, when the time came for Johnny to step into Heaven, Sheila was traumatized by his absence. Sheila had rejection and abandonment anxieties due to inconsistencies and lack of nurturing and love during her childhood, so Johnny's departure was, in itself, traumatic. He had been her rock. Now she was without her firm foundation. She didn't know how she could go on, but when she came to the Heartwork Retreat, she found a community of caring and loving women who helped her talk through the trauma of losing her husband, her anchor. Sheila rediscovered her roots that go down deep into Jesus. She is now drawing on her rich faith in Jesus Christ to help her through these lonely, dark times.

Sheila said,

> I attended a Heartwork Retreat. This changed my way of seeing the trauma of losing my hubby of 40 years. At the retreat, widows like me were heard by wonderful ladies who are also widows. The repeating of my story and their listening and validation was very helpful and eye opening. I will forever be grateful for the work, love, and kindness that they gave me at the retreat. I arrived thinking I wanted it (my life) to be over. I left singing with a smile on my face, feeling like I had a purpose to live. It isn't a cure or a fix-all. It is just a beautiful step in the right direction toward God's grace and healing. I realized that God had brought me to a sanctuary of healing, a place of restoration, and a place to start again. Am I healed or "over it"? Absolutely not. But I now understand the process and know that there are beautiful Christian ladies who understand and care. That, in my eyes, is HUGE!! I came broken in spirit, battered by life, exhausted from carrying it by myself. I left with a mended spirit, a bandaged life, and a community of

women who relieved the stress and brought me rest and peace. Do I still have waves of grief? Yes. Do I still miss him? Yes. But the tools they gave me and continue to give me when I lean in, are priceless. I am thankful beyond measure for these beautiful ladies, their hearts of love, and their desire to bring healing and hope to widows everywhere.

CHAPTER NINE

MOVING FORWARD IN GRIEF

Once the trauma has been healed, it will be important for the **PARTICIPANT** to bear in mind a heavenly perspective on earthly suffering. It would be wonderful if they could exhale, relax and say, "Whew! I'm glad that's over!" But even though the trauma is now behind them, the grief journey still lies ahead. Jesus will be close at their side and will not leave them defenseless, as Bruce McLeod says in *Take Heart: A Widowed Man's Guide to Growing Stronger*:

> There really is a kingdom of darkness. Satan really does want to steal from, kill, and destroy me (John 10:10). The adversary really does prowl around like a roaring lion. He is looking for someone to devour (1 Peter 5:8). He especially hates Jesus-lovers. Our world really is a world at war.
>
> The good news is this: if I resist the devil (stand firm against him), he will flee from me. How do I resist him? First, I deny the accusation, after all, it's a lie

from the father of them. Then, I state the truth of what Jesus says about me.

When moving forward in grief, one's focus is important. As Dr. Paul Meier says in *Don't Lose Heart: A Widow's Guide to Growing Stronger*:

> If I am able to focus my eyes on Jesus, I will see things from an eternal perspective. I used to get angry, even with God, when I experienced disappointments and crises. I would be surprised and even shocked by them, as though somehow, I was entitled to a calamity-free life. I also tended to "catastrophize"—to assume the worst scenario—when trouble did arise. Now I can step back a bit, gain perspective and realize that God will help me through whatever comes my way. In fact, He will even use it to grow me up!

Mary Beth Woll goes on to say:

> This new kind of perspective emerges from repeatedly choosing to focus our eyes on Jesus. What a beautiful alternative to constantly paying attention to ourselves and our problems! It is only natural for humans to be somewhat self-absorbed. It is easy to turn our gaze inward and concentrate on our own needs and wants.
>
> When the Bible uses the term "fix," it is not referring to a casual glance, but instead purposely turning away from one thing to focus on something else. It is difficult to fix our eyes on our own problems and on Jesus at the same time, but deliberately pondering His insight into our predicaments is very practical, since obsessing about our struggles doesn't work anyway.

Jesus has better solutions to our problems. (*Don't Lose Heart! A Widow's Guide to Growing Stronger*, p. 38).

A BIBLICAL PERSPECTIVE FOR YOUR GRIEF

Though your trauma has been healed, your grief walk continues through the Valley of the Shadow of Death. Here are some Scriptures and encouraging thoughts to help you keep your eyes on Jesus, your Good Shepherd, who tends to you, His hurting sheep.

God is close to the brokenhearted.
- Psalm 34:18 - "The Lord is close to the brokenhearted and saves those who are crushed in spirit."

God offers us comfort and healing so that we, in turn, can offer comfort to other sufferers.
- 2 Corinthians 1:3-4 – "Praise be to the God and Father of our Lord Jesus Christ, the Father of compassion and the God of all comfort, who comforts us in all our troubles, so that we can comfort those in any trouble with the comfort we ourselves have received from God."

God is with us and will strengthen us, so we do not need to be afraid.
- Isaiah 41:10 – "So do not fear, for I am with you; do not be dismayed, for I am your God. I will strengthen you and help you, I will uphold you with my righteous right hand."

God knows that we have been deeply wounded. Though it takes time, He will heal us.
- Psalm 147:3 – "He heals the brokenhearted and binds up their wounds."

- Jeremiah 17:14 – "Heal me, O Lord, and I will be healed; save me, and I will be saved, for you are the one I praise."

Jesus suffered rejection and pain more than any man, so He can understand our suffering. Because of this, we know that Jesus is a compassionate Healer.
- Isaiah 53:3-5 – "He was despised and rejected by men, a man of sorrows and familiar with suffering… By His wounds we are healed."

- Hebrews 4:15 – "For we do not have a high priest who is unable to sympathize with our weaknesses, but we have one who has been tempted in every way, just as we are—yet was without sin."

God can turn even our grief and trauma into something that will work for our good and the blessing of others.
- Romans 8:28 – "And we know that in all things God works for the good of those who love him, who have been called according to his purpose."

- Genesis 50:20 – "You intended to harm me, but God intended it for good to accomplish what is now being done, the saving of many lives."

Even though times of peace may be rare during grief, we can still trust that God promises that He will eventually bring us through to experience His peace. Through prayer, meditating on God's Word, and fellowship with other believers, God can once again restore His supernatural peace in our hearts and minds, even amid distress.
- John 14:27 – "Peace I leave with you; my peace I give you. I do not give to you as the world gives. Do not let your hearts be troubled and do not be afraid."

- Philippians 4:6-7 – "Do not be anxious about anything, but in everything by prayer and petition, with thanksgiving, present your requests to God. And the peace of God, which transcends all understanding, will guard your hearts and your minds in Christ Jesus."

FINAL ENCOURAGEMENT

Heartwork is an effective tool to heal the traumatic memories surrounding the death of a loved one. Through the power of the Holy Spirit and the support of the Christian community, we can be free from the prison of fear. As we "bear one another's burdens" (Galatians 6:2), the Bible reassures us that no pain or trauma is beyond God's ability to heal, because with God, all things are possible (Matthew 19:26).

ADDENDUM

HEARTWORK RETREAT

ORIENTATION FOR HEARTWORK LEADERS AND INTERCESSORS

HEARTWORK LEADERS AND INTERCESSORS WILL MEET TOGETHER BEFORE PARTICIPANTS ARRIVE.

Note: In order to participate in Heartwork, it is essential that Heartwork **LEADERS** and **INTERCESSORS** have been healed from their own trauma. Otherwise, they will not be as effective with **PARTICIPANTS** and may even experience vicarious trauma by hearing the **PARTICIPANT'S** story.

PREPARE OUR HEARTS WITH A WORSHIP SONG OR TWO.

PREPARE OUR HEARTS THROUGH INNER HEALING SCRIPTURES

Proverbs 20:5

- The purposes of a person's heart are deep waters, but a man of understanding draws them out.

Psalm 51:10

- Create in me a pure heart, O God, and renew a steadfast spirit within me.

Psalm 139:23-24

- Search me, God, and know my heart; test me and know my anxious thoughts. See if there is any offensive way in me and lead me in the way everlasting.

2 Corinthians 10:4-5

- The weapons we fight with are not the weapons of the world. On the contrary, they have divine power to demolish strongholds. We demolish arguments and every pretension that sets itself up against the knowledge of God, and we take captive every thought to make it obedient to Christ.

PREPARE OUR HEARTS THROUGH PRAYER.

Invite the Holy Spirit to work in each of us and our **PARTICIPANTS** today.

The following prayers are part of Heartwork and will help you prepare yourself for what God wants to do through you today.

Armor of God Prayer

From Ephesians 6: 10-17

I take up the Belt of Truth.
Thank You that Your Word is Truth.
You are the Way, the Truth, and the Life.

I put on the Breastplate of Righteousness.
I thank You that I am the Righteousness
of God in Christ Jesus.

I put on the Shoes of the Preparation
of the Gospel of Peace.
I choose to go where You want me to go.

I take up the Shield of Faith
with which I quench all the fiery darts
of the wicked one.

I put on the Helmet of Salvation.
Thank you, Lord, that You have given me
the very Mind of Christ.

I take up the Sword of the Spirit,
which is the Word of God, sharper than any two-edged sword,
dividing the soul and spirit.

In Jesus' Mighty Name,

Amen

The Inner Healing Prayer

By Dr. Rita Bennett

Dear Father God,

I yield my will to You.

I give You permission to go to any level within me to heal, cleanse, and restore according to Your truth. To the best of my ability, I invite You to be my Lord, unconditionally. Please be Lord of my subconscious, as well as my conscious mind.

I renounce every false teaching and attitude and ask You to cleanse and protect me with Jesus' blood. I cast down every wrong imagination and everything that exalts itself against the knowledge of God, and I take every thought captive to the obedience of the Lord Jesus Christ. (2 Corinthians 10:5).

Thank You, Lord God.

In Jesus' Name,

Amen

Prepare ourselves

Please be sure that you have read chapters 6 and 7 in the Heartwork book. They are foundational.

When the **Leader** creates the Timeline in the **Participant's** book, it is important to leave space between the lines of the recorded memories. As the **Participant** begins to integrate the trauma into their consciousness, they will remember more details. It's not our purpose to create a comprehensive Timeline, but to allow for peripheral memories that begin to integrate.

Because the **Participant's** brain will be working hard to connect left-brain events with right-brain emotions, it is critical that the **Intercessor** prays silently, and the **Leader's** voice is the only one the **Participant** hears.

As the **Intercessor** prays silently during the session, they write down any impressions they receive from the Holy Spirit. The

INTERCESSOR will have an opportunity to share these impressions in prayer with the **PARTICIPANT** at the end of the session. The **LEADER** will record the **INTERCESSOR'S** final prayer on the **PARTICIPANT'S** phone.

Meet your team – **LEADERS**, **INTERCESSORS**, and **PARTICIPANTS** have been prayerfully grouped. The **LEADER** and **INTERCESSOR** will meet at the beginning of orientation. Please pray together before your **PARTICIPANT** arrives.

You will receive a Schedule of Events at the orientation. You will need a pen and a "*Heartwork*" book. The **PARTICIPANT** will bring their own book for the **LEADER** to write in. (Otherwise, ask for a book.)

Then meet the **PARTICIPANT** when they arrive at the registration table. While you wait, get a nametag for yourself if you don't already have one. Enjoy the mix-and-mingle as the **PARTICIPANTS** begin to gather, creating a warm and welcoming atmosphere.

Enjoy the moving of the Holy Spirit as the retreat **LEADERS** guide you through the weekend. We will see miraculous changes!

Suggested Heartwork Retreat Schedule

Friday

2:00	Leaders' and Intercessors' Training and Prayer
4:30	Participants arrive
5:00	Opening Prayer and Dinner for everyone
6:00	Worship
6:30	Heartwork Session 1
8:30	Wrap-up and Closing Prayer
	Optional Bonfire

Saturday

9:00	Breakfast and Announcements
9:45	Prayer
10:00	Heartwork Session 2
12:00	Lunch and Free Time
1:30	Heartwork Session 3
3:15	Significant Snackage
3:30	Ministry Time
	Testimonies, Communion, and Prayer
5:00	Dismissal

Heartwork Brief Intervention

By Mary Beth Woll, MA, LMHC, CTP, and Linda Smith, BS

For this process, you need a **Leader**, an **Intercessor**, and a **Translator**. The **Leader** facilitates this process. The **Intercessor** prays silently for this session and writes down any insights the Holy Spirit gives them. They shares these insights with the **Leader** and the **Participant** at the end of the prayer time.

The **Participant** tells their story of the crisis. The **Translator** interprets this story to the **Leader** and the **Intercessor**. Both the **Leader** and the **Translator** write down the major elements of the **Participant's** story, leaving room between lines for additional information.

The **Leader** asks clarifying questions. Both the **Leader** and the **Translator** take notes:

- What was happening immediately before the crisis?
- What happened immediately after the crisis, up to the present?
- What was the worst part of the crisis?
- When you think of that worst part, where do you feel it in your body?

The **LEADER** asks, "Would you like Jesus to help you heal from the pain of this crisis?"

If not, the **LEADER** can still help them by repeating their story to them and telling them how sorry you are that it happened. Offer to pray for them. This completes your ministry to them.

If yes, the **LEADER** asks the **PARTICIPANT** if they would be willing to pray the following Inner Healing Prayer with the **LEADER**. If so, the **TRANSLATOR** reads the following prayer to the **PARTICIPANT** to invite Jesus into the process.

> *Dear Father God,*
>
> *I yield my will to You. I give You permission to go to any level within me to heal, cleanse, and restore according to Your truth. To the best of my ability, I invite You to be my Lord, unconditionally. Please be Lord of my subconscious, as well as my conscious mind.*
>
> *I renounce every false teaching and attitude and ask You to cleanse and protect me with Jesus' blood. I cast down every wrong imagination and everything that exalts itself against the knowledge of God, and I take every thought captive to the obedience of the Lord Jesus Christ. (2 Corinthians 10:5).*
>
> *Thank you, Lord God.*
>
> *In Jesus' Name,*
>
> *Amen*

The **Translator** then explains that they will now read the **Participant's** story back to them.

Next, the **Leader** instructs the **Participant** to ask Jesus where He was during the crisis. Wait patiently for the Holy Spirit to speak to the **Participant**. Ask them to tell you what they hear from the Holy Spirit.

The **Leader** asks, "How was that for you when you heard your own story from me?"

Then the **Leader** asks, "Now, when you think of the worst part of your story, where do you feel it in your body?"

The **Leader** writes down their response and compares it to where the **Participant** first felt it in their body.

If time allows, repeat the above process. If not, the **Leader** and **Intercessor** pray for the **Participant** and share what the Holy Spirit has been speaking to them about them.

Close with this Sealing Prayer:[6]

"That which has been done in Jesus' Name and to His glory cannot be undone. I decree this and seal this prayer in the Name of the Father, Son, and Holy Spirit."

---

[6]   Dr. Rita Bennett, Emotionally Free Course, Basic Prayer Book, p. 55.

About the Authors

Linda Smith, BS   **Mary Beth Woll, MA, LMHC, CTP**

Mary Beth and Bob were married for almost 39 years before the Lord took him home. Bob and Mary Beth were co-music ministers for 20 years. Together they have four children and eight grandchildren. Mary Beth has a master's degree in counseling/psychology and worked as a clinical therapist with Meier Clinics for 19 years before becoming Co-Director of The Widows Project.

Linda was married to Kirby for 37 years. They have two children and six grandchildren. She comes from a background in education—both Christian and secular. She taught at every age level and has led several widows' support groups before becoming Co-Director of The Widows Project.

BIBLIOGRAPHY

American Psychological Association. (n.d.). *Narrative Exposure Therapy.* APA. Retrieved February 6, 2025, from https://www.apa.org

Bennett, Rita. *Emotionally Free Course.* Christian Renewal Association, 1982.

Dobson, James C. *When God Doesn't Make Sense.* Tyndale House Publishers, 1993. Excerpted in *When God Doesn't Make Sense* [Booklet]. Focus on the Family, Australia, 2009.

Gray, Derwin L. "What we don't grieve won't leave." YouVersion Bible App, YouVersion, 10 Sept. 2024. www.bible.com

Holmes, T.H., & Rahe, R.H. (1967). *The Social Readjustment Rating Scale.* Journal of Psychosomatic Research, 11(2), 213–218.

Leaf, Caroline. *Switch on Your Brain: The Key to Peak Happiness, Thinking, and Health.* Baker Books, 2013.

McLeod, Bruce, and Chris Taylor: *Take Heart!: A Widowed Man's Guide to Growing Stronger.* The Widows Project, 2021.

Seamands, David A. *Healing of Memories*, Victor Books, 1985.

Smith, Linda, and Mary Beth Woll, editors. *Take Courage!: Growing Stronger after Losing Your Spouse.* The Widows Project, 2021.

The Holy Bible, New International Version, Zondervan, 1978.

The Holy Bible, New International Version. 1978 ed., Zondervan, 1978, www.biblegateway.com. Accessed February 7, 2025.

Van der Kolk, Bessel A. *The Body Keeps the Score: Brain, Mind, and Body in the Healing of Trauma.* Viking, 2014.

Woll, Mary Beth, and Linda Smith. *Don't Lose Heart!: A Widow's Guide to Growing Stronger.* The Widows Project, 2020.

Woll, Mary Beth, and Paul Meier, MD. *Growing Stronger: 12 Guidelines Designed to Turn Your Darkest Hour into Your Greatest Victory.* Morgan James, 2013.

Heartwork Journal

___
___
___
___
___
___
___
___
___
___
___
___

BOOKMARKS

Armor of God Prayer
From Ephesians 6: 10-17

I take up the Belt of Truth.
Thank You that Your Word is Truth. You are the Way, the Truth, and the Life.

I put on the Breastplate of Righteousness.
I thank You that I am the Righteousness of God in Christ Jesus.

I put on the Shoes of the Preparation of the Gospel of Peace.
I choose to go where You want me to go.

I take up the Shield of Faith
with which I quench all the fiery darts of the wicked one.

I put on the Helmet of Salvation.
Thank you, Lord, that You have given me the very Mind of Christ.

I take up the Sword of the Spirit,
which is the Word of God, sharper than any two-edged sword, dividing the soul and spirit.

In Jesus' Mighty Name,

Amen

The Inner Healing Prayer
By Dr. Rita Bennett

Dear Father God,

I yield my will to You.

I give You permission to go to any level within me to heal, cleanse, and restore according to Your truth. To the best of my ability, I invite You to be my Lord, unconditionally. Please be Lord of my subconscious, as well as my conscious mind.

I renounce every false teaching and attitude and ask You to cleanse and protect me with Jesus' blood. I cast down every wrong imagination and everything that exalts itself against the knowledge of God, and I take every thought captive to the obedience of the Lord Jesus Christ.
(2 Corinthians 10:5).

Thank You, Lord God.

In Jesus' Name,

Amen

Touches a previous wound which

Reminds us of a painful experience resulting in

Inward reactivity which unconsciously

Grips us emotionally

Generating an

Exacggerated

Response to our present situation.

www.ingramcontent.com/pod-product-compliance
Lightning Source LLC
LaVergne TN
LVHW061554070526
838199LV00077B/7037